Original Scroll Saw Shelf Patterns

Patrick Spielman
& Loren Raty

D1613686

Sterling Publishing Co., Inc. New York

Library of Congress Cataloging-in-Publication Data

Spielman, Patrick E.
    Original scroll saw shelf patterns / by Patrick Spielman & Loren
Raty.
      p. cm.
    Includes index.
    ISBN 0-8069-8714-6
    1. Jig saws. 2. Shelving (Furniture) 1. Raty, Loren.
II. Title.
TT186.S666   1993
684.1′6—dc20   92-39062
                                                   CIP

Edited by Rodman Pilgrim Neumann

10 9 8 7 6 5 4 3 2 1

Published in 1993 by Sterling Publishing Company, Inc.
387 Park Avenue South, New York, N.Y. 10016
© 1993 by Patrick Spielman and Loren Raty
Distributed in Canada by Sterling Publishing
% Canadian Manda Group, P.O. Box 920, Station U
Toronto, Ontario, Canada M8Z 5P9
Distributed in Great Britain and Europe by Cassell PLC
Villiers House, 41/47 Strand, London WC2N 5JE, England
Distributed in Australia by Capricorn Link Ltd.
P.O. Box 665, Lane Cove, NSW 2066
Manufactured in the United States of America
All rights reserved

Sterling ISBN 0-8069-8714-6

Contents

Color section follows p. 64.

Metric Conversion

Inches to Millimetres and Centimetres

MM—millimetres   CM—centimetres

Inches	MM	CM	Inches	CM	Inches	CM
⅛	3	0.3	9	22.9	30	76.2
¼	6	0.6	10	25.4	31	78.7
⅜	10	1.0	11	27.9	32	81.3
½	13	1.3	12	30.5	33	83.8
⅝	16	1.6	13	33.0	34	86.4
¾	19	1.9	14	35.6	35	88.9
⅞	22	2.2	15	38.1	36	91.4
1	25	2.5	16	40.6	37	94.0
1¼	32	3.2	17	43.2	38	96.5
1½	38	3.8	18	45.7	39	99.1
1¾	44	4.4	19	48.3	40	101.6
2	51	5.1	20	50.8	41	104.1
2½	64	6.4	21	53.3	42	106.7
3	76	7.6	22	55.9	43	109.2
3½	89	8.9	23	58.4	44	111.8
4	102	10.2	24	61.0	45	114.3
4½	114	11.4	25	63.5	46	116.8
5	127	12.7	26	66.0	47	119.4
6	152	15.2	27	68.6	48	121.9
7	178	17.8	28	71.1	49	124.5
8	203	20.3	29	73.7	50	127.0

Introduction

Making and selling the wall shelves from the pattern designs in this book is an excellent income-producing activity for all scroll-saw owners. The shelves, which generally require only about a single square foot of material, will sell for between $35 to $50 each. Just making shelves for the fun of it as gifts to friends and family is economical and self-satisfying. The good part is, everyone has use for them.

This book contains complete, full-size patterns that can be copied and applied directly to the wood. Some are more complex than others, but all are by and large equally popular. No one design seems to be more popular than another. Surprisingly, those painted in solid colors are almost as popular and purchased as quickly as those made from hardwoods with natural finishes.

Basic Materials

All of the patterns are designed to be made from material ¼ inch in thickness (Illus. 1). Hardwood plywood is an ideal choice. Various species are available, with oak and birch probably the easiest to find locally. However, walnut, cherry, mahogany, and even exotic woods such as teak are made into plywood, but they are expensive and difficult to find.

Avoid fir and luan plywoods. They splinter and do not finish well. The actual shelf piece and bracket support should be made

Illus. 1. Shelf cut from ¼-inch-thick solid wood (left), and plywood (right). Note the dark contrasting core of the plywood, which may or may not be objectionable.

from plywoods that have two good faces because these parts are visible on both surfaces. Or you can use solid woods for these parts if they are available to you in ¼-inch thicknesses. In fact, the entire shelf can be made from solid wood. Solid woods actu-ally look best for shelves that will receive natural finishes. Use oak, walnut, cherry, mahogany, birch, or soft maple for natural-finished shelves. Other suitable solid woods include pine, poplar, basswood, and the like for painted finishes.

Copying the Patterns

Since most of the shelves are actually larger than the single-page size of this book, most patterns must be presented for you in parts or sections. Once they are all copied, they are then easily butted or joined together to form the full profile shape of the pattern. Consequently, a single shelf pattern may extend across two to as many as four or five continuous pages depending upon the size of the overall pattern. A full-size pattern is given for every part of the shelf project. After using one or two patterns, you'll quickly see how easy they are to use.

Occasionally, because of space limitations a simple shelf part may be given as just a half-pattern. However, a full pattern can be developed quickly and very easily. Simply make a paper fold on the pattern's given center line. Use a scissors and cut the pattern line out in paper doll fashion.

Today, the use of the modern office copy machine is the fastest and quickest way to copy or reproduce the patterns directly from this book. Once you have a paper pattern copy you can apply it directly to the surface of your wood.

Applying Patterns

Applying the patterns to the surfaces of the wood is best done with temporary bonding spray adhesive (Illus. 2) or brush-on rubber cement. These work great, but if you've never used either of these techniques before, test each out on scrap.

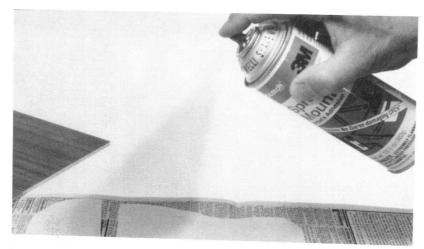

Illus. 2. Spraying a light mist to the back of a pattern copy. The newspaper catches the overspray.

First, roughly cut around each pattern part of the pattern with a scissors. Of the two kinds of adhesives, we recommend the spray type designed especially for making temporary and repositionable bonds. We use a 3M product called Scotch™ Temporary Spray Mount™ Artists Adhesive #6065. Always apply your adhesive to the back of the pattern only, not directly onto the wood.

Wait a few seconds and then press the pattern(s) onto the surface of the wood (Illus. 3). You are now ready to begin sawing with a perfect, clear pattern to follow.

After all sawing is completed, you can peel the paper pattern off of the wood very easily (Illus. 4). The temporary spray mounting adhesive leaves practically no residue whatsoever on the wood and does not inhibit subsequent finishing. If you have used rubber cement, you may have to remove some of it from the wood. Just rub it off with your fingers.

Illus. 3. Join two or more pattern sections together, as necessary, directly on the wood to complete the full pattern. Once aligned, press them down.

Illus. 4. After sawing is completed, the pattern will peel cleanly and easily from the surface of the wood.

Stack-Sawing

Stack-sawing is the process of placing two or more pieces one on top of another and sawing them all at one time (Illus. 5 and 6). This is an especially good production technique when making more than one shelf of the same pattern. Stack-cutting saves considerable time and should be employed when possible—especially when you're in the business.

Be sure you do not exceed the cutting capacity or capability of your scroll saw. Some machines cut considerably better than others. Always be sure to use good sharp blades, and your saw table must be perfectly square to your blade. Two to six (or more) layers can be cut all at once in about the same amount of time and effort it takes to cut just one piece.

Illus. 5. Preparation for stack-sawing four complete shelves at one time. Note that the straight lines of the shelf and the bracket patterns are aligned at the straight edges of the workpiece.

Illus. 6. Stack-sawing. Here six layers of ¼-inch-thick solid wood are being sawn all at once, producing six identical parts.

The optimum number of layers you can saw at one time will depend upon a number of variables, including the following: (1) the sawing thickness capacity of your saw and its capability for accuracy; (2) the size, kind, and sharpness of the blade; (3) the kind of material to be cut. Some plywoods have excessive layers and more glue than others, which takes its toll on blade sharpness very quickly. In general, use the widest and coarsest blade that will give you a smooth cut and still permit making the curves necessary. Use maximum blade tension.

Tip: When stack-sawing, you may want to slip in a layer of tagboard or file-folder stock so you can simultaneously cut out a full-size template.

Fastening Layers Together

Fastening the layers together for stack-sawing can be done in a variety of ways. Perhaps the easiest and quickest is simply to nail them together to make a tight pad (*see* Illus. 5). You can also use masking tape as a wrap or place double-faced tape between layers. You can also hold two layers of ¼-inch-thick stock together with a ⅜-inch staple driven by a household staple gun. You will quickly determine which technique works best for you, and then sawing multiple pieces is easy.

Drilling Saw Gates

Saw blade entry holes or saw gates will need to be drilled, as necessary, for making the interior cutouts. When drilling these blade threading holes, be sure to have the work piece(s) supported over a piece of scrap to minimize splintering around the holes as the bit exits through the bottom surface.

Sawing

This should be easy. Cut directly on the line. You should not experience any force-feeding sensation, just a smooth resistance-free cutting action. Hard feeding and a smell of heat or burning wood will indicate trouble, likely a dull blade, and poorly cut edges are sure to result. Stop immediately; change blades, and reduce the number of layers or obtain a different material altogether. When properly cut, the sawn surfaces will be very smooth and not require any sanding at all.

Assembly and Finishing

Remove the pattern (Illus. 4). Sand the face surfaces, front and back as necessary, to remove any fuzz or slight feathering that sometimes develops along the sawn edges. Use 120–150 grit sandpaper. A fairly worn piece of abrasive under your fingertips works better than a new, stiff sheet (*see* Illus. 7). Drill small holes for attaching the

Illus. 7. Parts of a typical shelf cut from ¼-inch solid mahogany, sanded and ready to assemble.

shelf and bracket pieces to the back. Use small brads or wire nails at least ⅝ inch in overall length. If you don't have a bit matching the size of your nails, cut the head off of a nail and use it as a bit. You'll be surprised how well it actually works. You may also want to test and try one of the new super-glues. They work especially well for attaching the brackets that support the shelves. They work very well and set fast. Any excess or squeeze-out is hardly visible under natural finishes. However, if you stain, glue spots are sure to show through, regardless of what kind of glue you use.

Applying the Finish

Apply the finish of your choice in brand or type. We recommend one or more light coats of an aerosol satin spray natural finish or spray-on pigmented colors, as you wish. Penetrating natural-oil finishes are also ideal and easy to use for elegant natural-looking finishes. When using such penetrating or Danish oil finishes you must always wipe off the excess oil from all surfaces. Otherwise, those surfaces with resins remaining on them become sticky.

Shelf Patterns

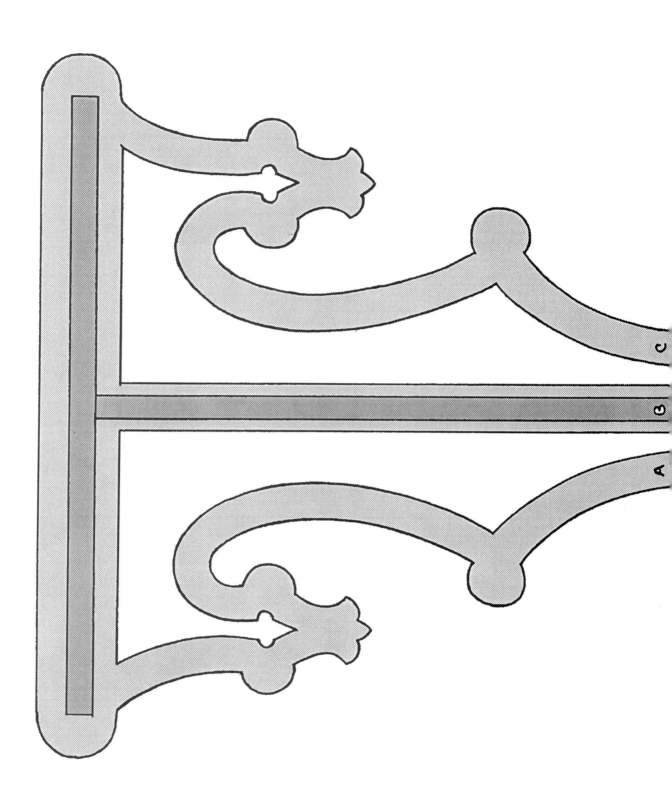

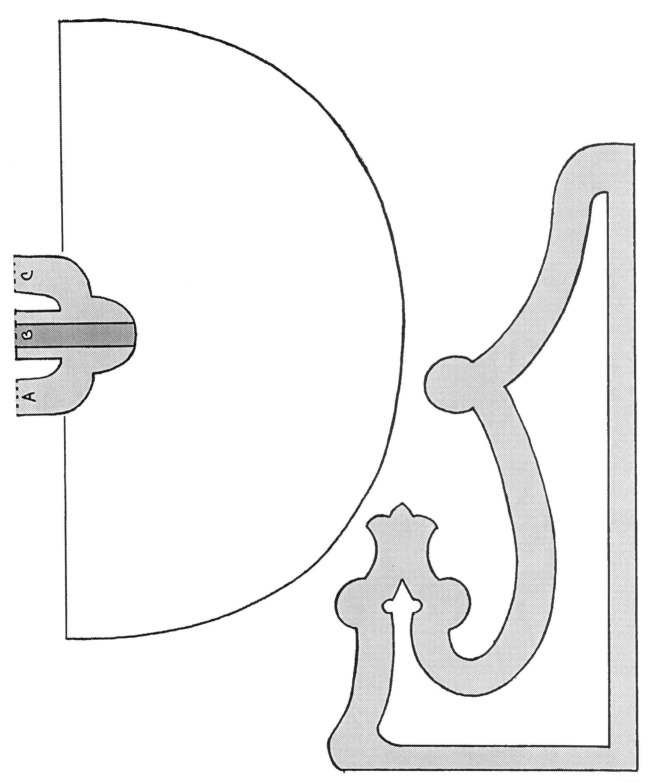

A B C

13

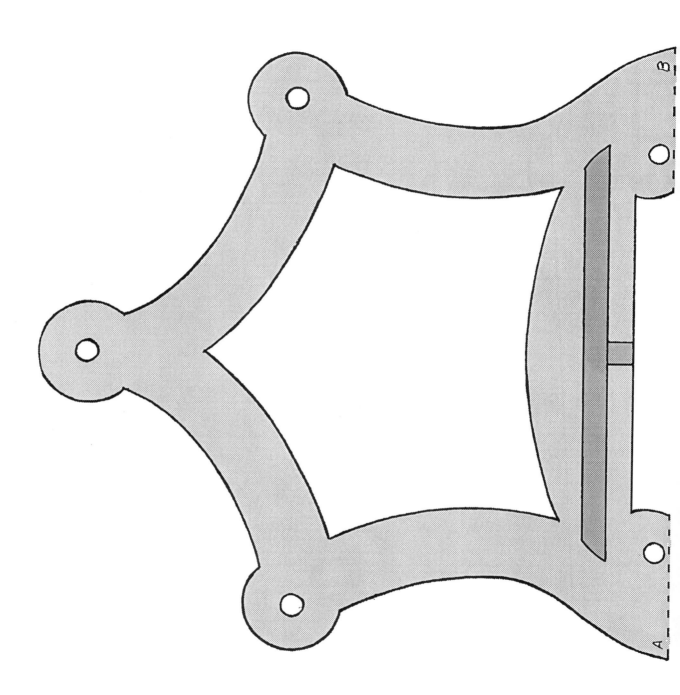

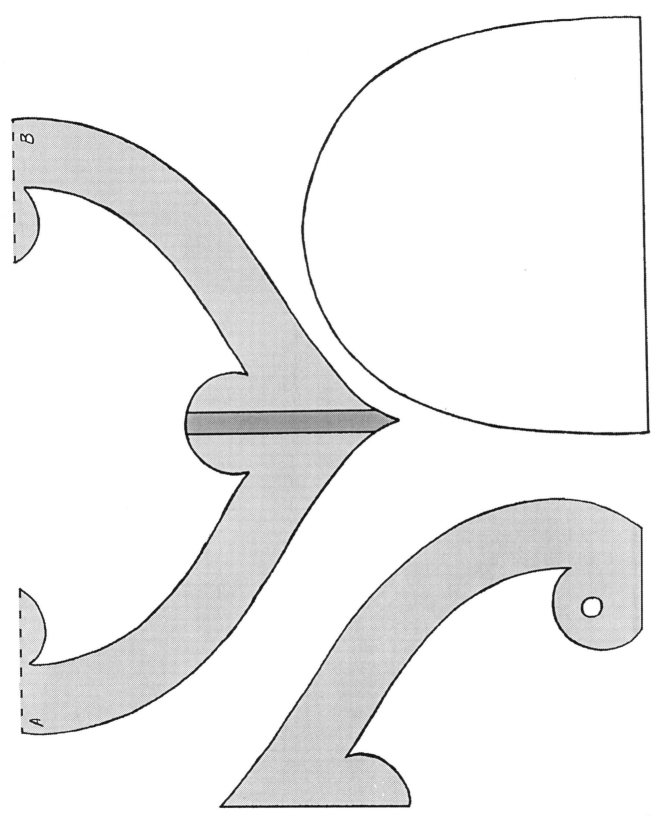

B

A

O

15

B

A

18

See page B of the color section.

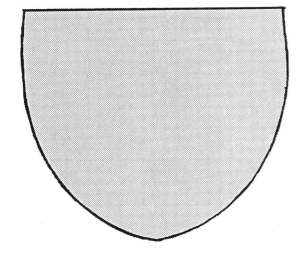

19

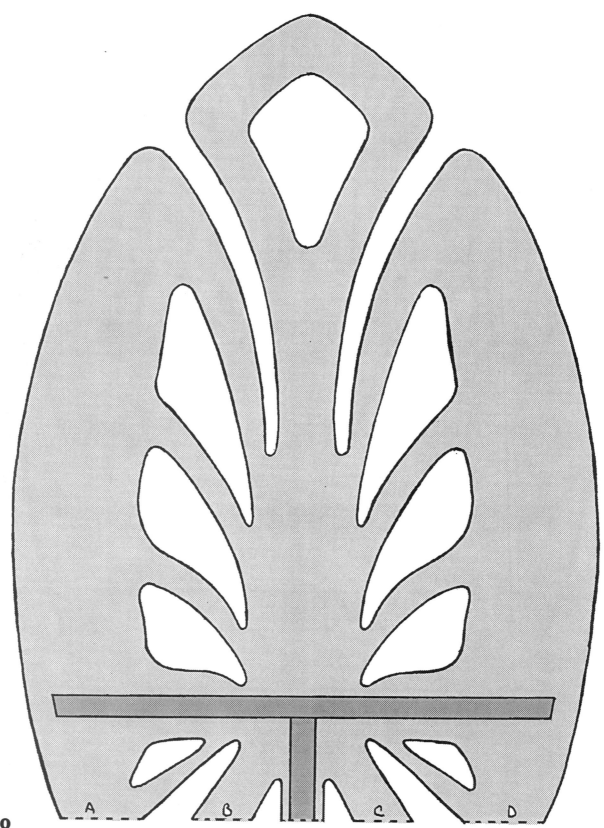

20

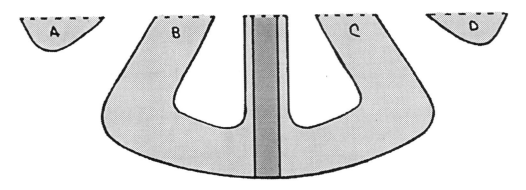

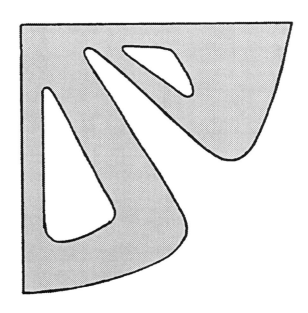

See page D of the color section.

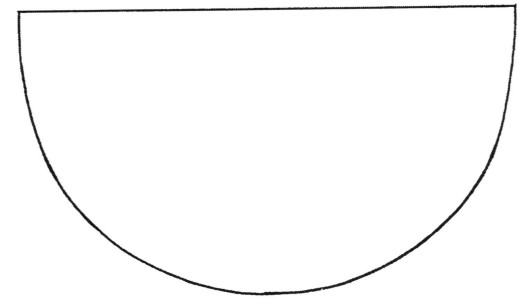

See page C of the color section.

C

B

A

HALF SHELF PATTERN

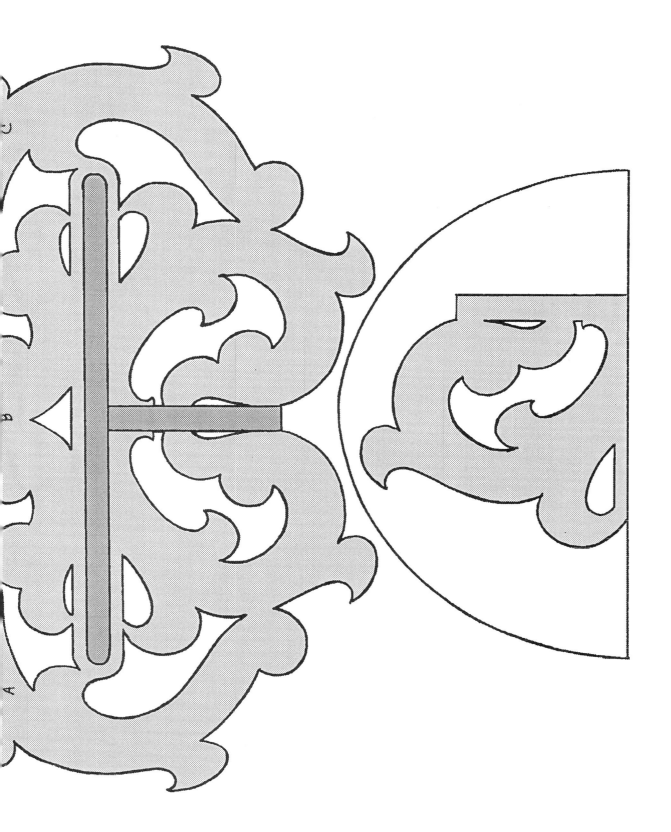

A   B

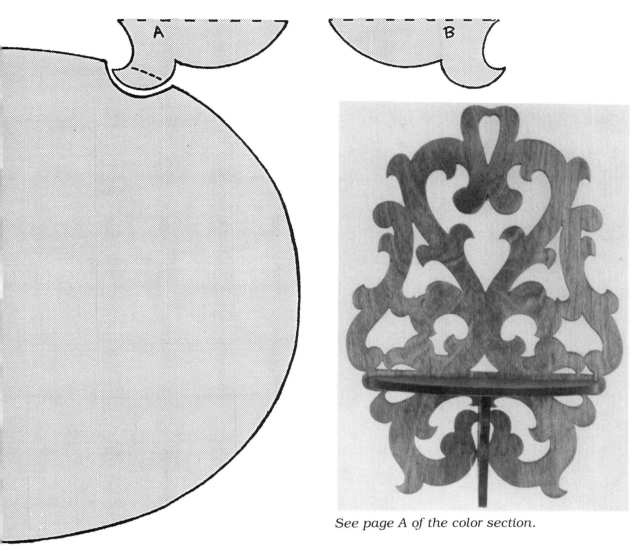

See page A of the color section.

See page D of the color section.

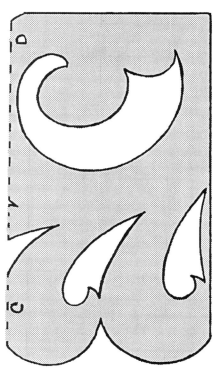

Photo and shelf template on following page.

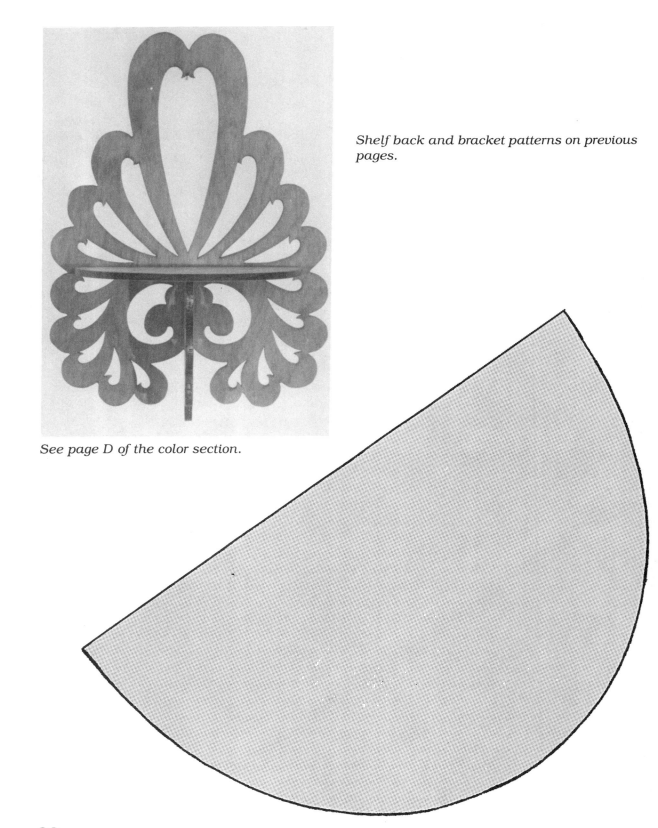

Shelf back and bracket patterns on previous pages.

See page D of the color section.

See page D of the color section.

Upper shelf and bracket
patterns and shelf back
pattern on following pages.

Photo, lower bracket and shelf patterns on previous page.

B

A

B

A

See page A of the color section.

37

38

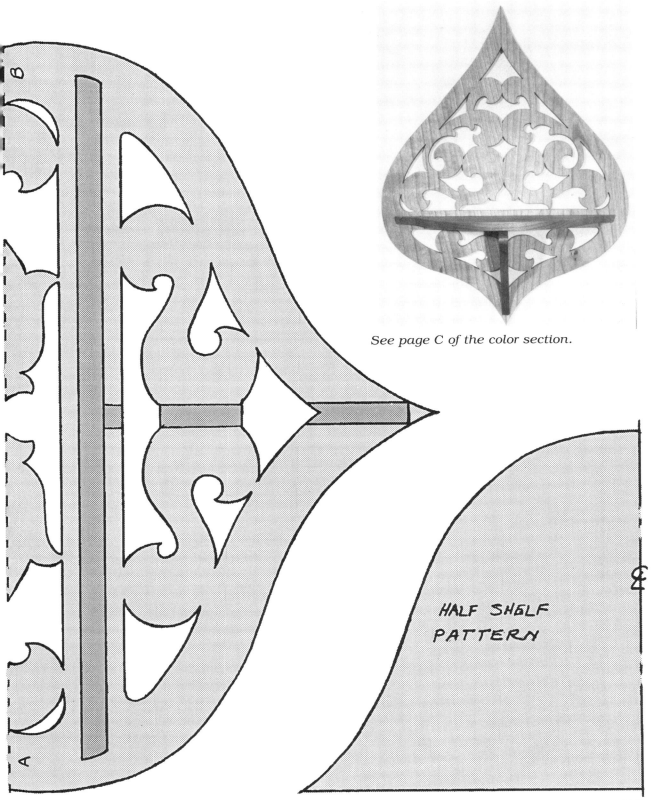

See page C of the color section.

HALF SHELF
PATTERN

B

A

A

B

HALF SHELF PATTERN

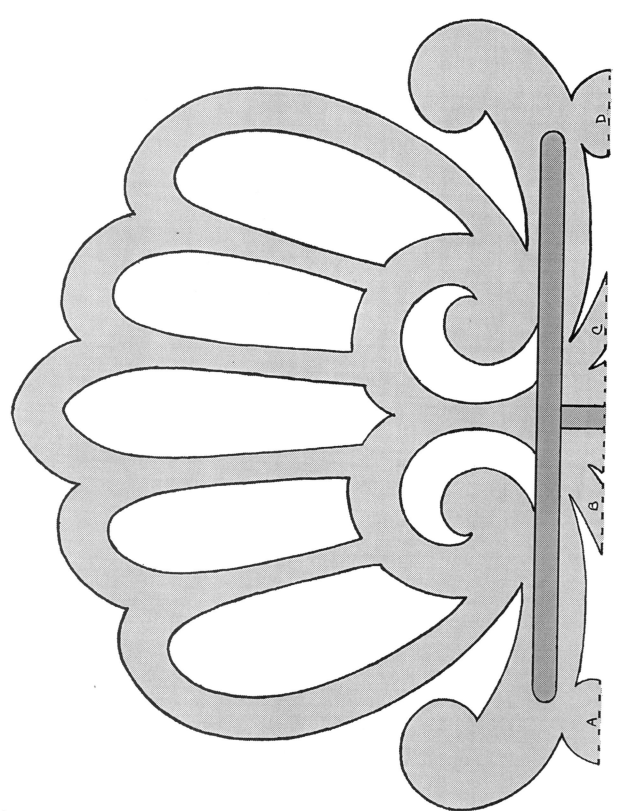

See page A of the color section.

HALF SHELF PATTERN

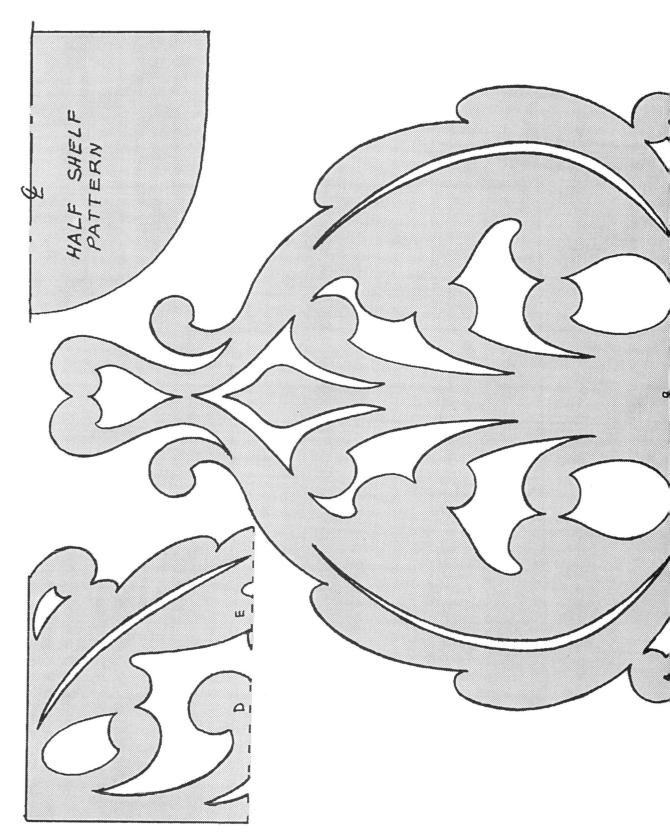

HALF SHELF
PATTERN

See page D of the color section.

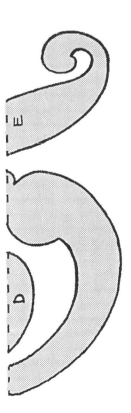

See page C of the color section.

49

HALF SHELF
PATTERN

53

54

See page D of the color section.

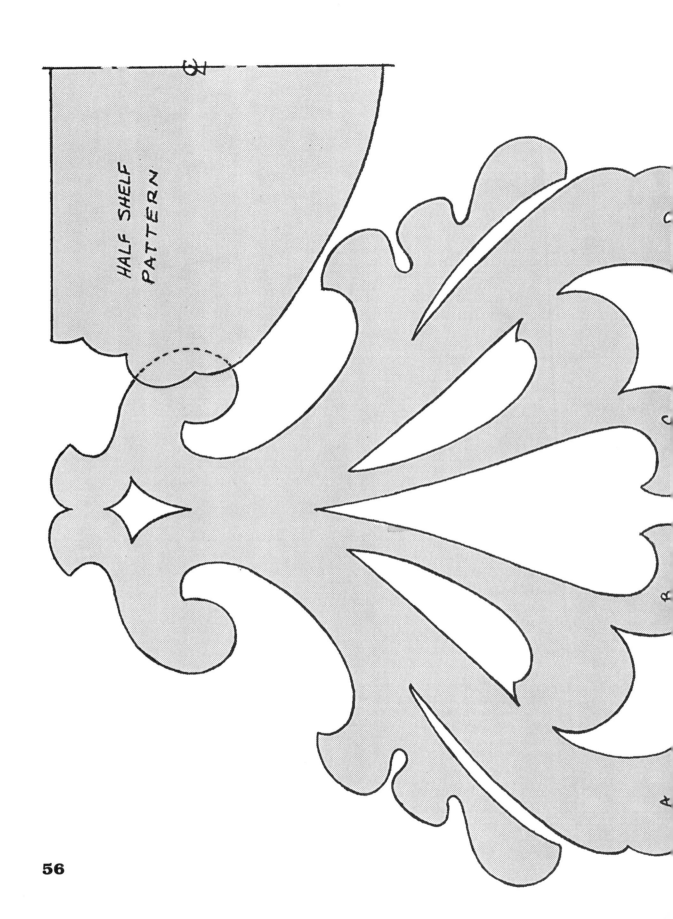

HALF SHELF
PATTERN

56

See page A of the color section.

HALF SHELF
PATTERN

59

A B C D E

60

61

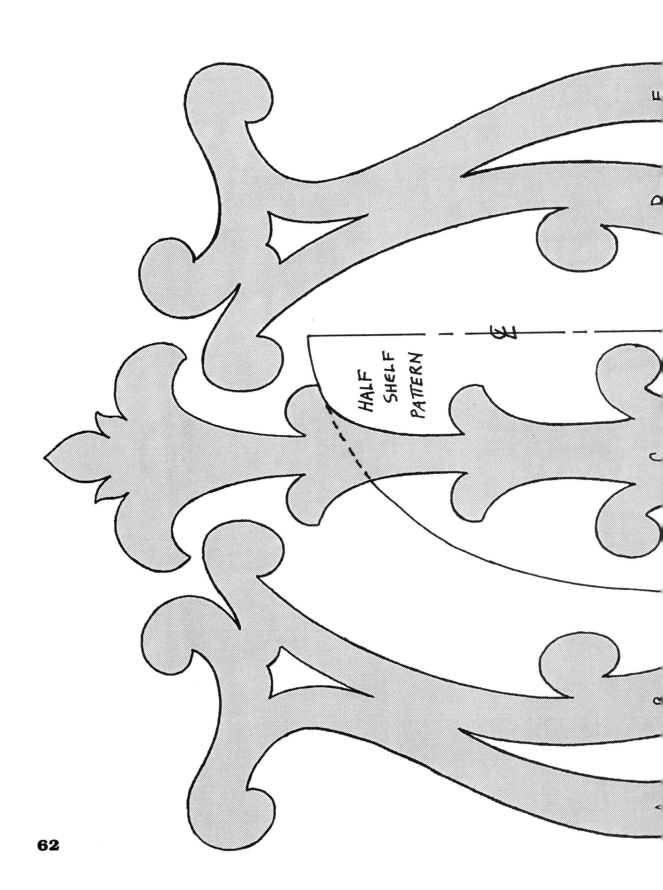

HALF
SHELF
PATTERN

62

See page B of the color section.

For pattern see pages 56–57.

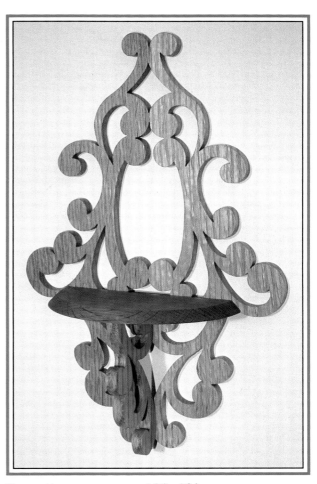

For pattern see pages 100–101.

For patterns see pages (left to right) 26–27, 44–45, 36–37.

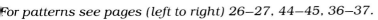

A

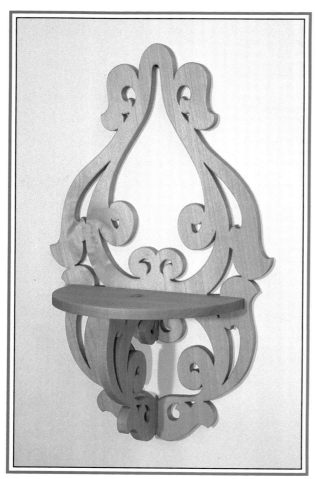

For pattern see pages 102–104.

For pattern see pages 18–19.

For patterns see pages (left to right) 62–63, 102–104, 114–115.

or pattern see pages 38–39.

For pattern see pages 84–85.

or patterns see pages (left to right) 48–49, 77–79, 22–23.

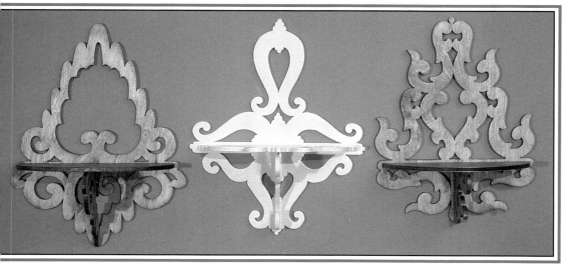

For patterns see pages (left to right) 28–29, 74–76, 30–32.

For patterns see pages (left to right) 92–95, 54–55, 33–35, 70–71.

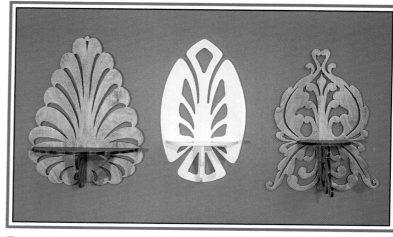

For patterns see pages (left to right) 66–67, 20–21, 46–47.

D

HALF SHELF
PATTERN

65

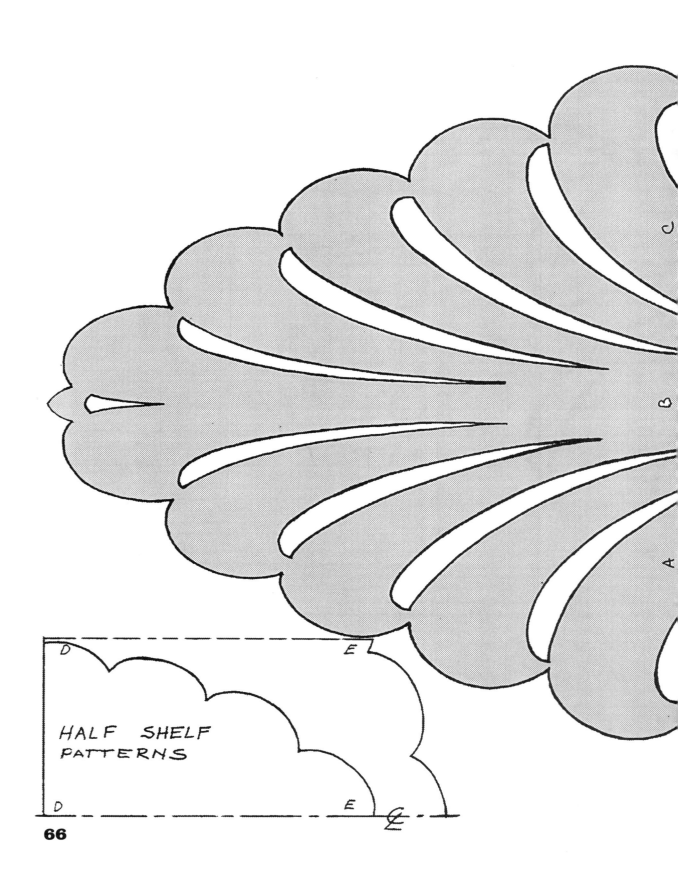

J

B

A

HALF SHELF
PATTERNS

D

E

D

E

₵

See page D of the color section.

67

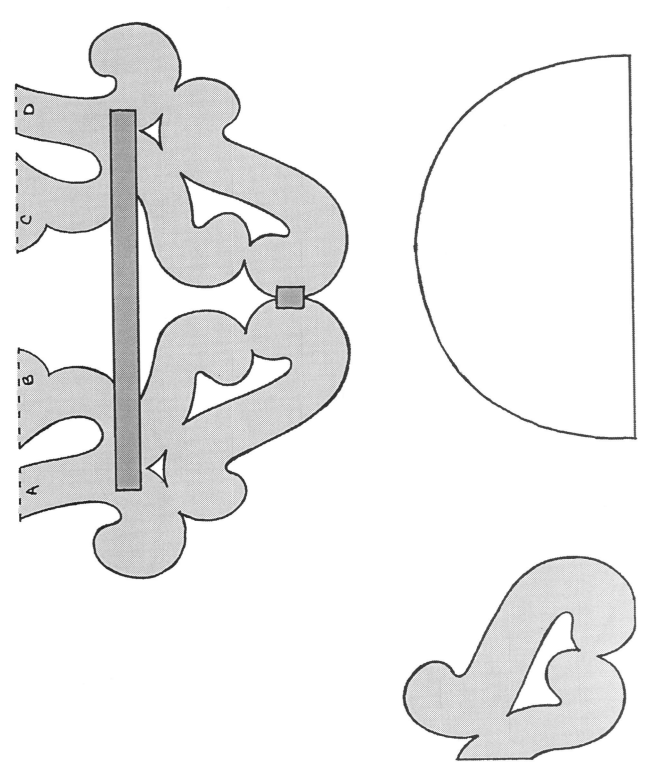

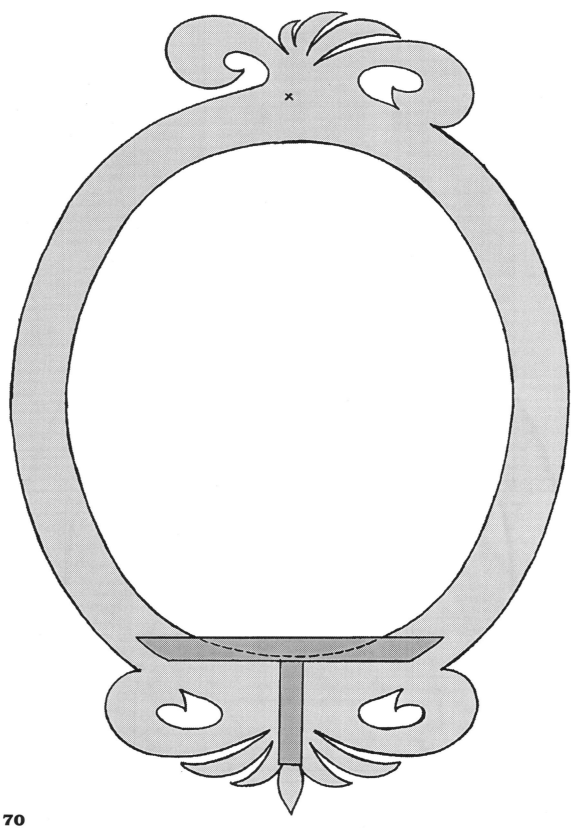

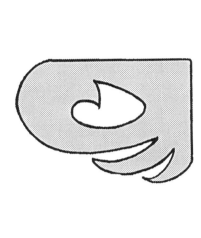

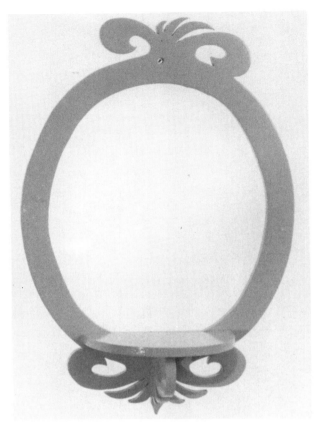

See page D of the color section.

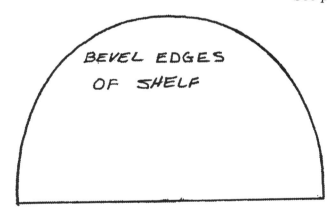

BEVEL EDGES
OF SHELF

A

B

C

D

HALF SHELF
PATTERN

₵

Photo, bracket and shelf patterns on following page.

See page D of the color section.

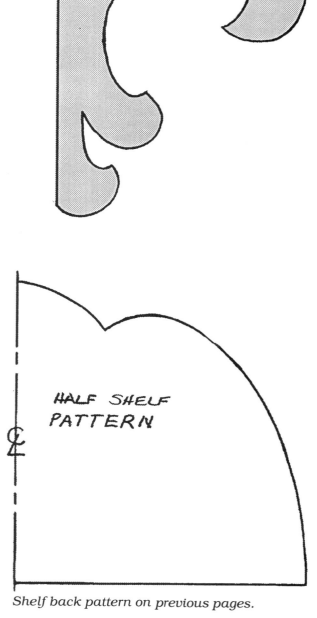

HALF SHELF
PATTERN

₵

Shelf back pattern on previous pages.

See page C of the color section.

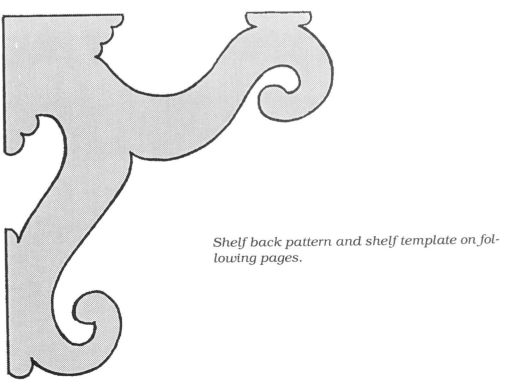

Shelf back pattern and shelf template on following pages.

Port Carling
Public Library

77

Photo and shelf bracket pattern on previous page.

79

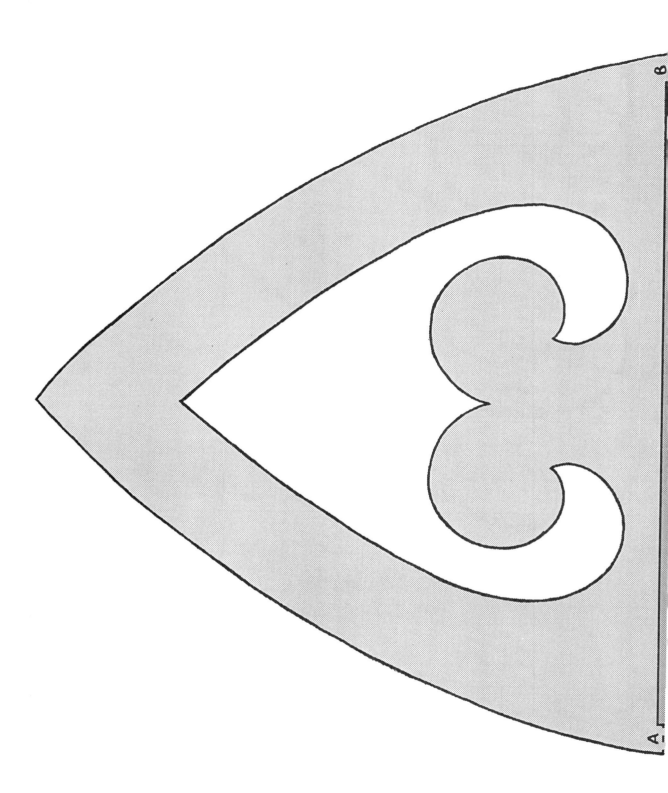

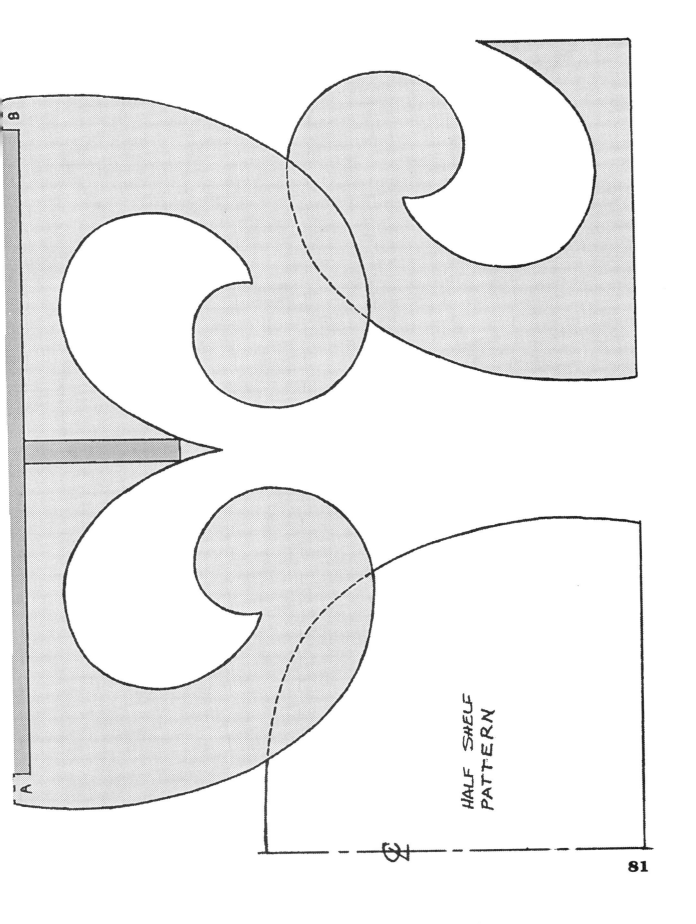

HALF SHELF
PATTERN

B

A

81

HALF SHELF
PATTERN

83

A B

See page C of the color section.

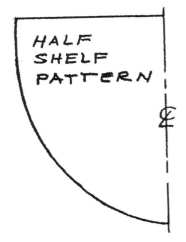

HALF
SHELF
PATTERN

85

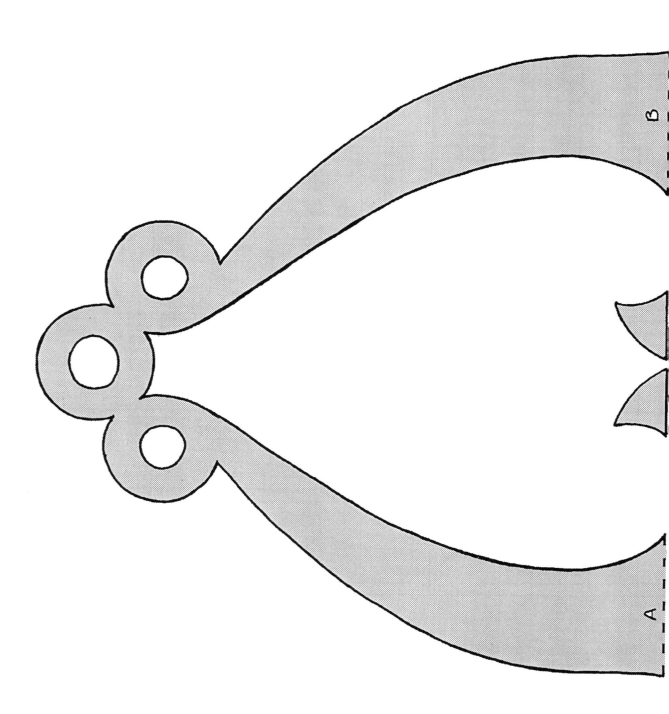

B

A

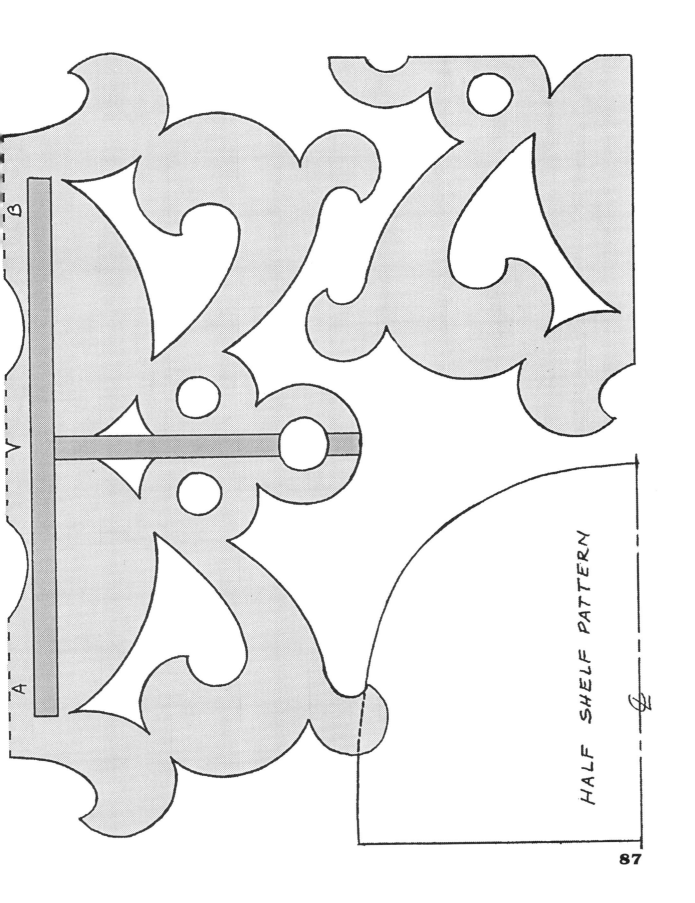

HALF SHELF PATTERN

A

B

87

B

A

BEVEL SHELF EDGES

HALF SHELF PATTERN

91

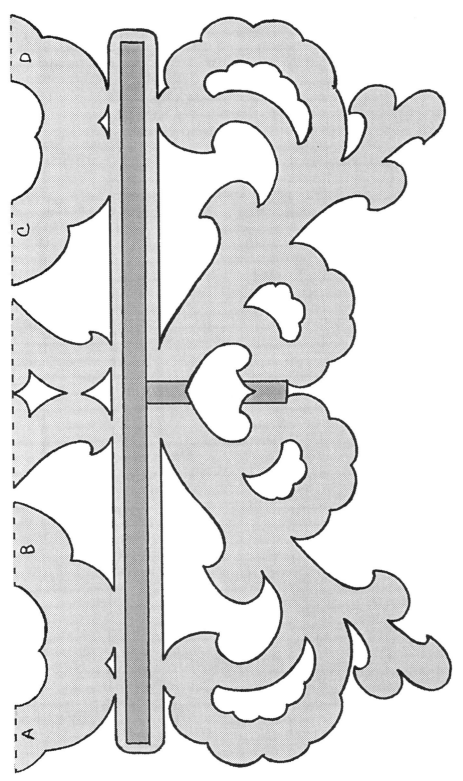

Photo, shelf and bracket patterns on following pages.

Shelf back pattern on previous pages.

See page D of the color section.

B

A

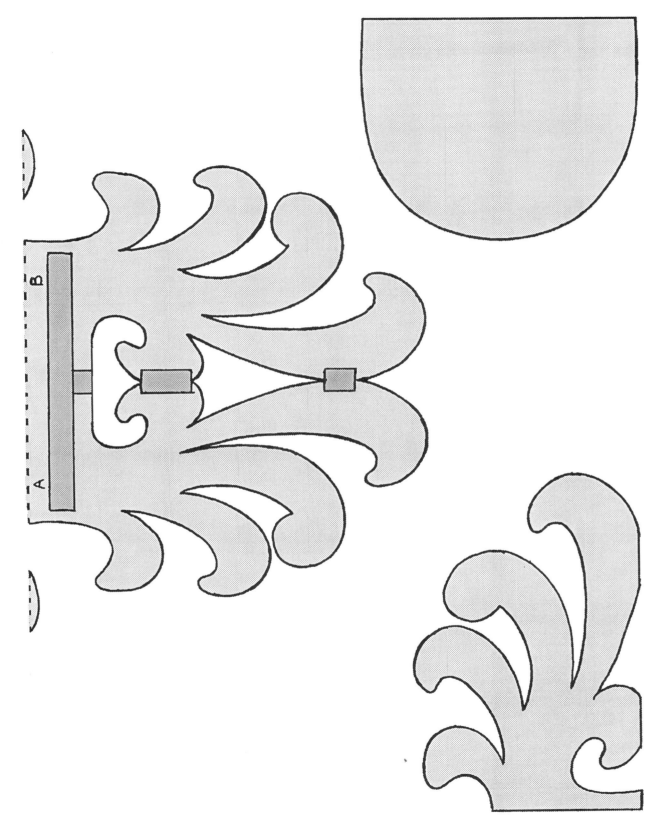

A

B

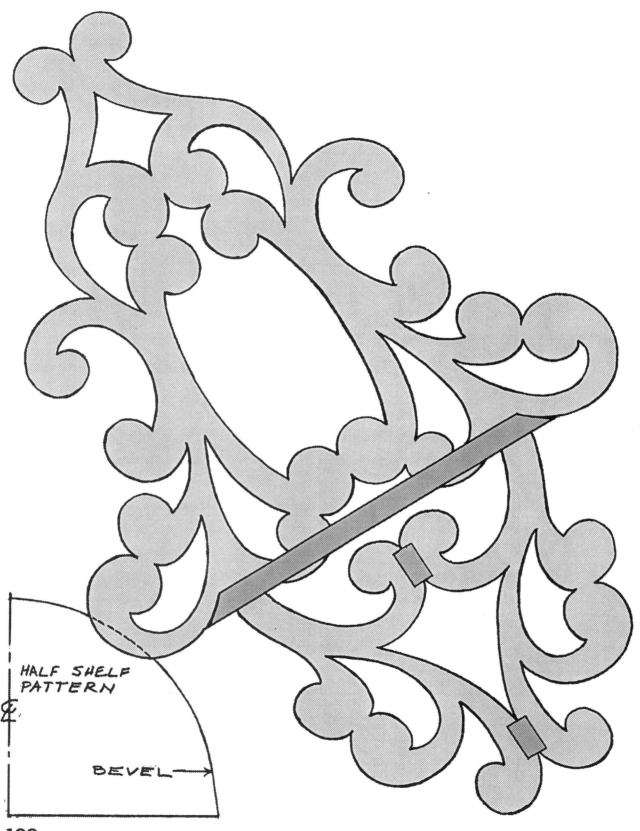

HALF SHELF
PATTERN

℄

BEVEL ⟶

100

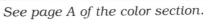

See page A of the color section.

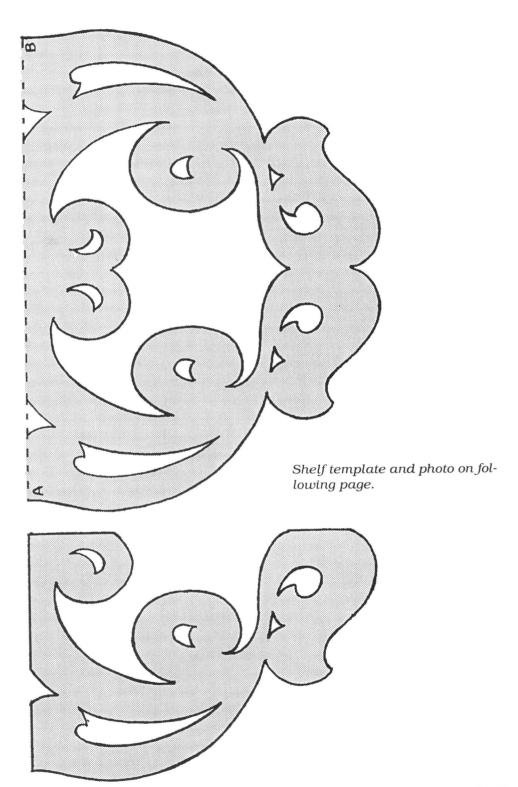

Shelf template and photo on following page.

103

Shelf back pattern and bracket pattern on previous pages.

See page B of the color section.

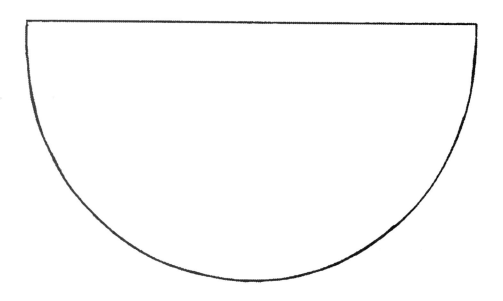

104

Shelf back and bracket patterns and shelf template on following pages.

Photo on previous page.

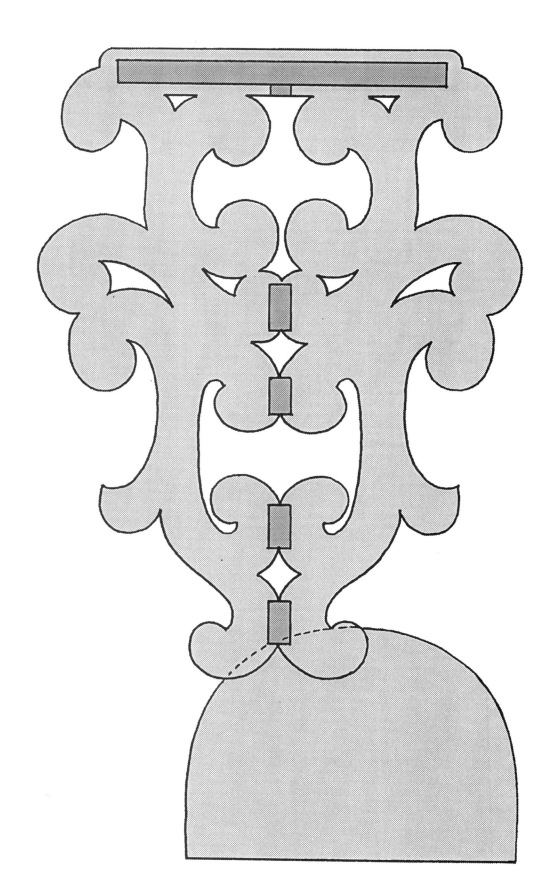

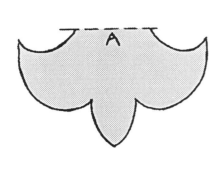

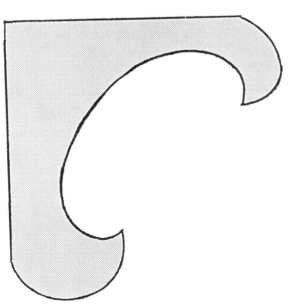

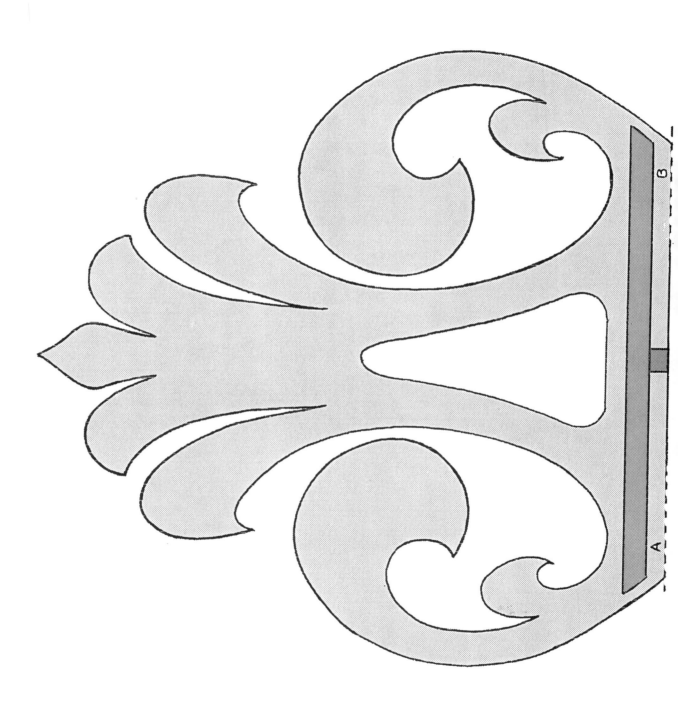

A

B

BEVEL
EDGE →

B

A

113

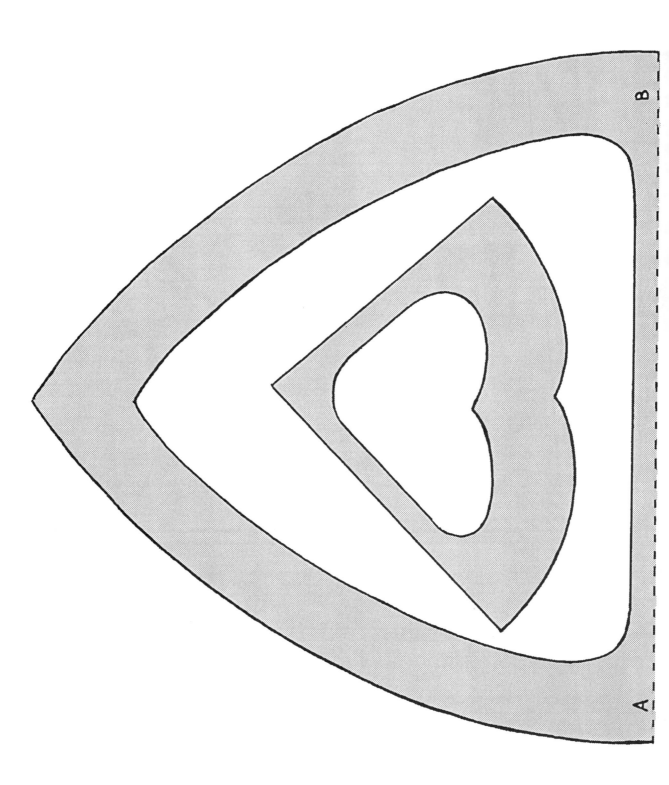

A

B

114

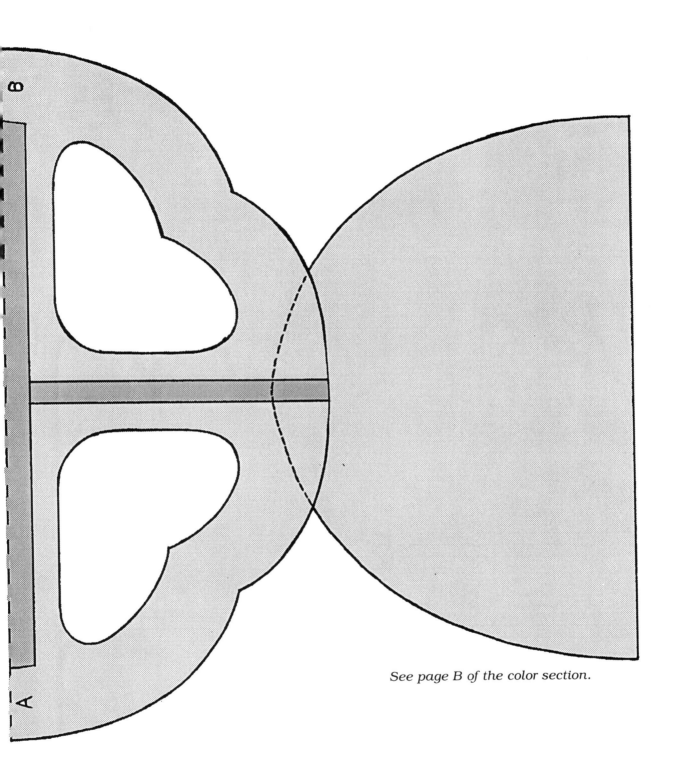

A

B

See page B of the color section.

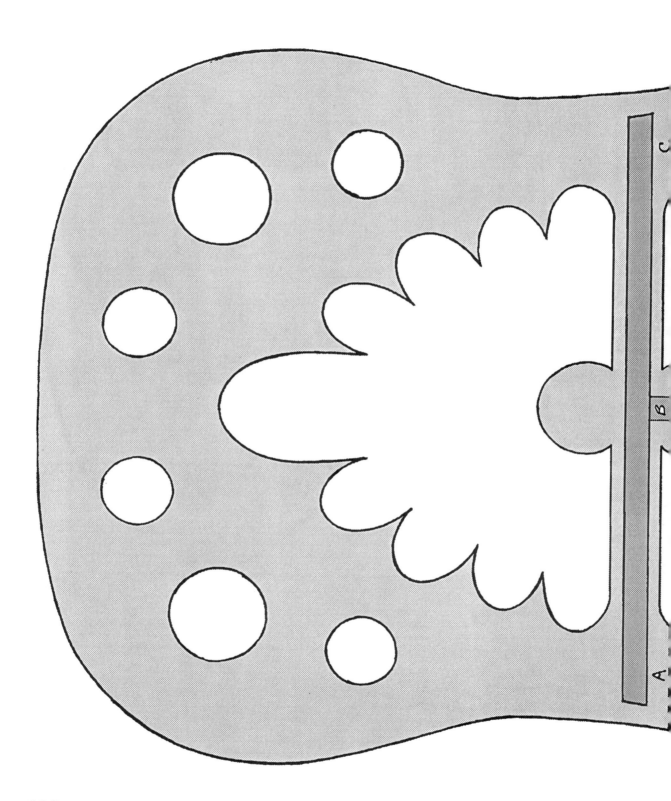

C

B

A

C

B

A

HALF SHELF
PATTERN

117

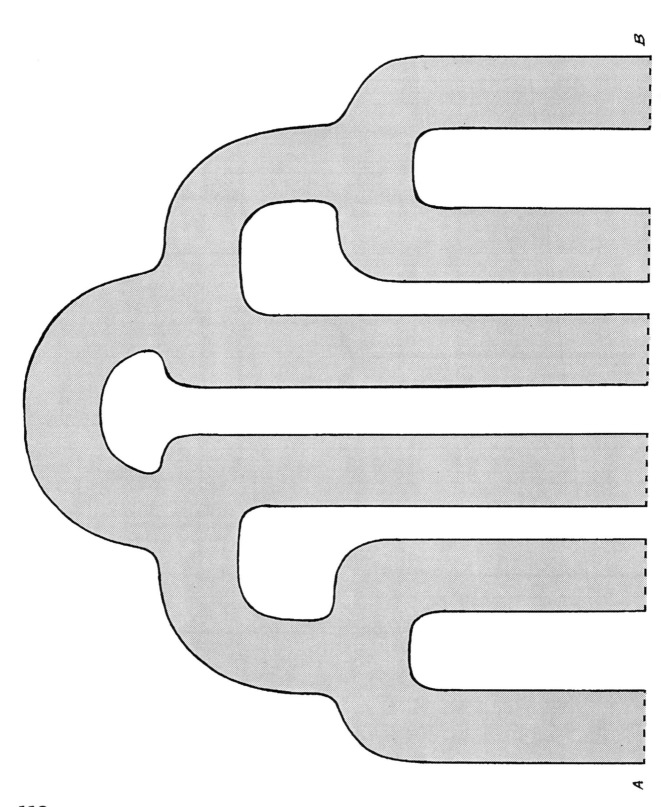

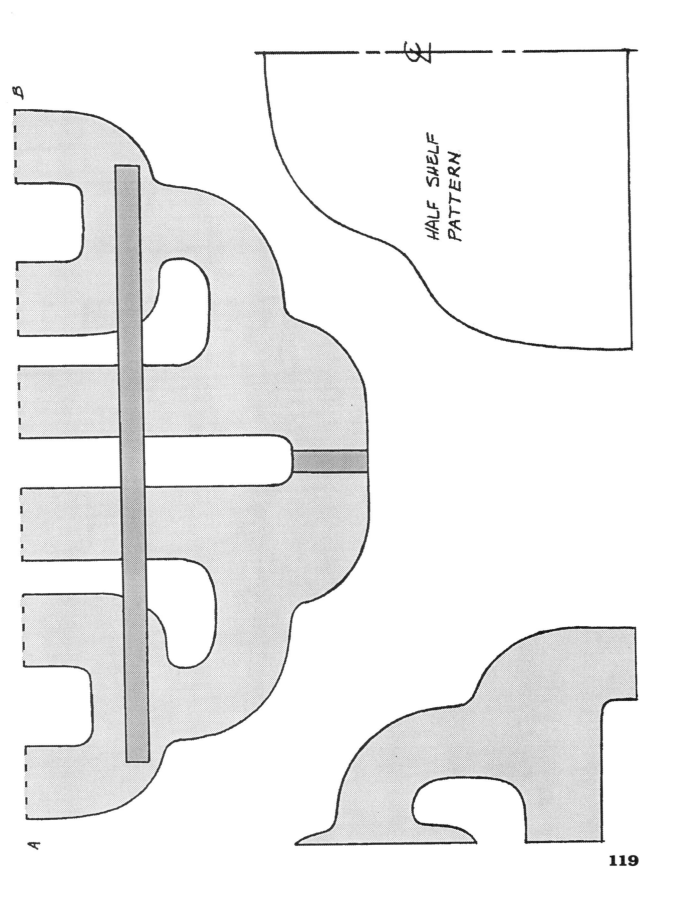

HALF SHELF
PATTERN

119

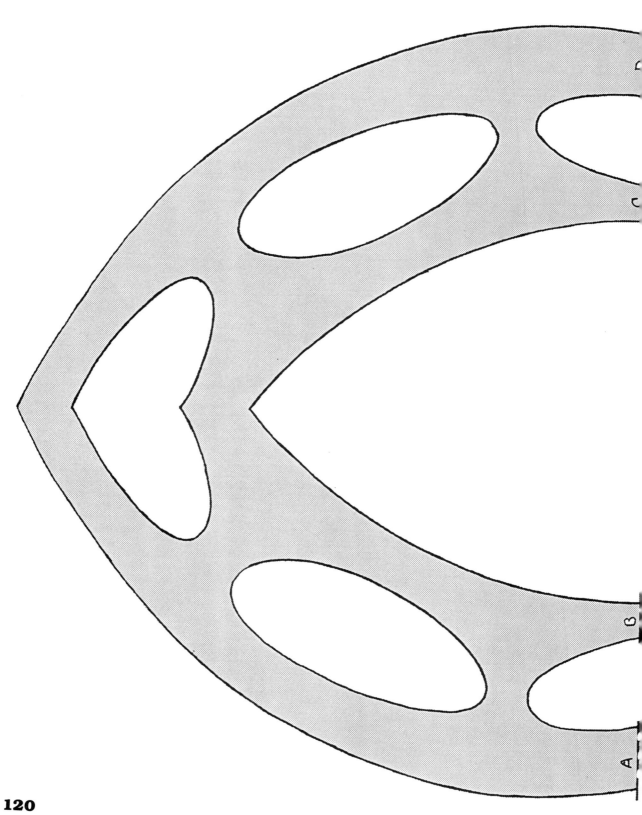

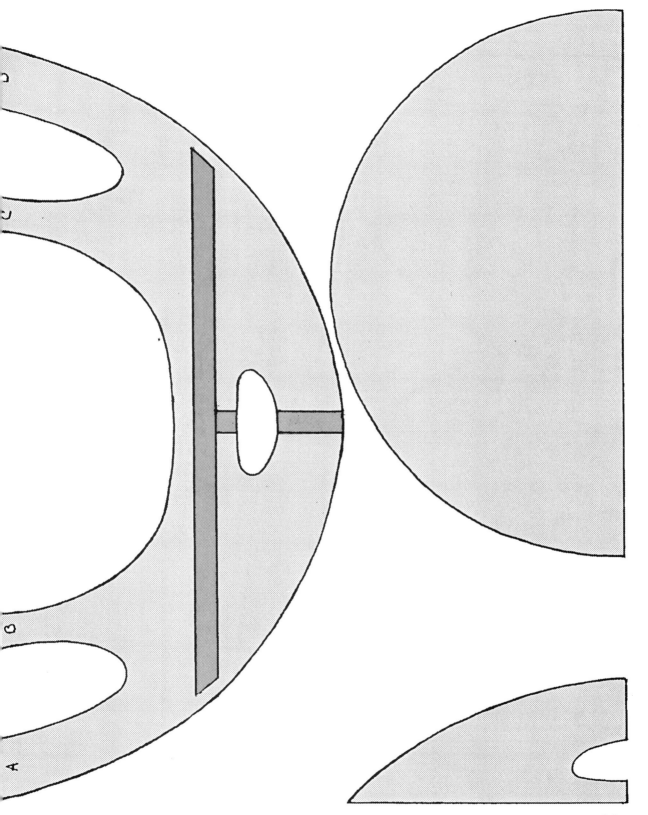

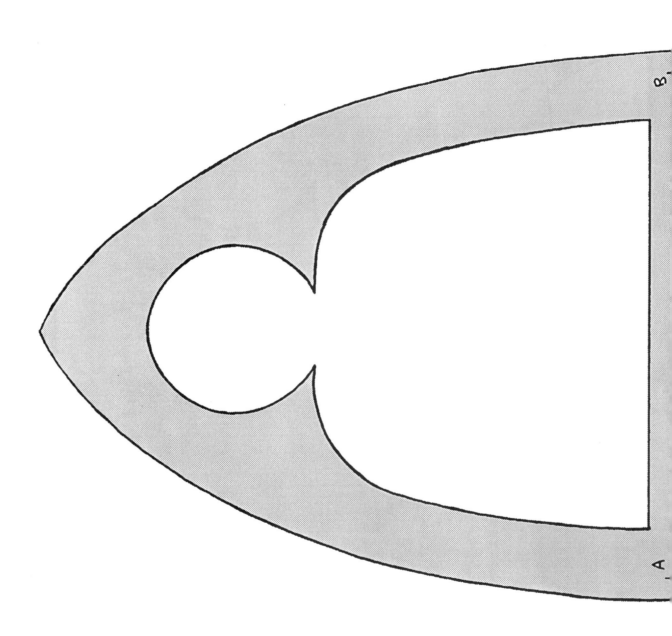

B

A

122

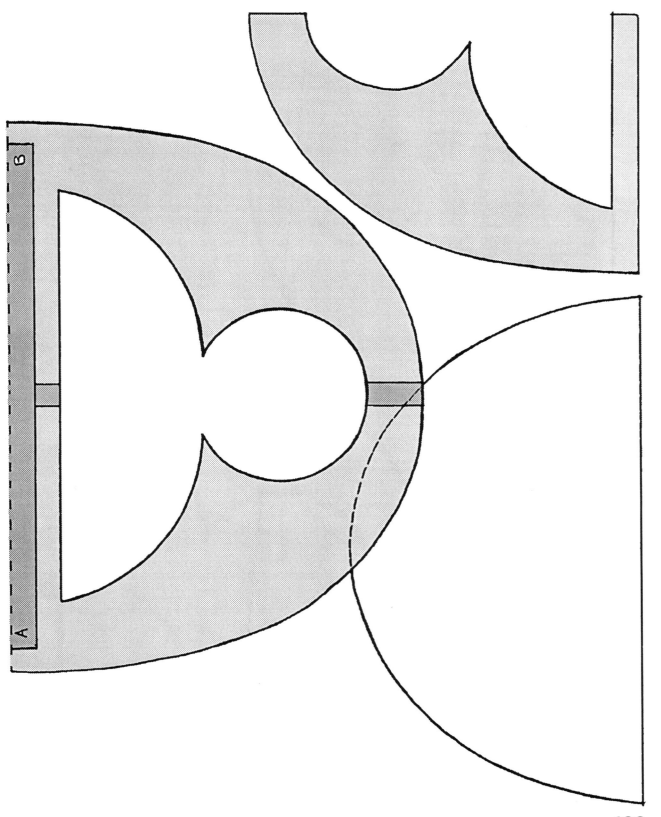

B

A

Current Books by Patrick Spielman

Alphabets and Designs for Wood Signs. 50 alphabet patterns, plans for many decorative designs, the latest on hand carving, routing, cutouts, and sandblasting. Pricing data. Photo gallery (4 pages in color) of wood signs by professionals from across the U.S. Over 200 illustrations. 132 pages.

Carving Large Birds. Spielman and renowned woodcarver Bill Dehos show how to carve a fascinating array of large birds. All of the tools and basic techniques that are used are discussed in depth, and hundreds of photos, illustrations, and patterns are provided for carving graceful swans, majestic eagles, comical-looking penguins, a variety of owls, and scores of other birds. Oversized. 16 pages in full color. 240 pages.

Carving Wild Animals: Life-Size Wood Figures. Spielman and renowned woodcarver Bill Dehos show how to carve more than 20 magnificent creatures of the North American wild. A cougar, black bear, prairie dog, squirrel, raccoon, and fox are some of the life-size animals included. Step-by-step, photo-filled instructions and multiple-view patterns, plus tips on the use of tools, wood selection, finishing, and polishing, help you bring each animal to life. Oversized. Over 300 photos. 16 pages in full color. 240 pages.

Classic Fretwork Scroll Saw Patterns. Spielman and colleague James Reidle provide over 140 imaginative patterns inspired by and derived from mid- to late-nineteenth-century scroll-saw masters.

This book covers nearly 30 categories of patterns and includes a brief review of scroll-saw techniques and how to work with patterns. The patterns include ornamental numbers and letters, beautiful birds, signs, wall pockets, silhouettes, a sleigh, jewelry boxes, toy furniture, and more. 192 pages.

Country Mailboxes. Spielman and colleague Paul Meisel have come up with the 20 best country-style mailbox designs. They include an old pump fire wagon, a Western saddle, a Dalmatian, and even a boy fishing. Simple instructions cover cutting, painting, decorating, and installation. Over 200 illustrations. 4 pages in color. 196 pages.

Gluing & Clamping. A thorough, up-to-date examination of one of the most critical steps in woodworking. Spielman explores the features of every type of glue—from traditional animal-hide glues to the newest epoxies—the clamps and tools needed, the bonding properties of different wood species, safety tips, and all techniques from edge-to-edge and end-to-end gluing to applying plastic laminates. Also included is a glossary of terms. Over 500 illustrations. 256 pages.

Making Country-Rustic Wood Projects. Hundreds of photos, patterns, and detailed scaled drawings reveal construction methods, woodworking techniques, and Spielman's professional secrets for making indoor and outdoor furniture in the distinctly attractive Country-Rustic style. Covered are all aspects of furniture making from choosing the best wood for the job to texturing smooth boards. Among the dozens of projects are mailboxes, cabinets, shelves, coffee tables, weather vanes, doors, panelling, plant stands, and many other durable and economical pieces. 400 illustrations. 4 pages in full color. 164 pages.

Making Wood Bowls with a Router & Scroll Saw. With master craftsman Carl Roehl, Spielman has come up with a completely new approach to creating decorative bowls with scroll-saw rings, inlay work, fretted edges, and much more. Over 200 illustrations. 8 pages in color. 168 pages.

Making Wood Decoys. A clear step-by-step approach to the basics of decoy carving. This book is abundantly illustrated with close-up photos for designing, selecting, and obtaining woods; tools; feather detailing; painting; and finishing of decorative and working decoys. Six different professional decoy artists are featured. Photo gallery (4 pages in full color) along with numerous detailed plans for various popular decoys. 164 pages.

Making Wood Signs. Designing, selecting woods and tools, and every process through finishing are clearly covered. Hand-carved, power-carved, routed, and sandblasted processes in small to huge signs are presented. Foolproof guides for professional letters and ornaments. Hundreds of photos (4 pages in full color). Lists sources for supplies and special tooling. 148 pages.

Realistic Decoys. Spielman and master carver Keith Bridenhagen reveal their successful techniques for carving, feather texturing, painting, and finishing wood decoys. Details that you can't find elsewhere—anatomy, attitudes, markings, and the easy step-by-step approach to perfect delicate procedures—make this book in-

valuable. Includes listings for contests, shows, and sources of tools and supplies. 274 close-up photos. 8 pages in color. 232 pages.

Router Basics. With over 200 close-up step-by-step photos and drawings, this valuable overview will guide the new owner as well as provide a spark to owners for whom the router isn't the tool they turn to most often. Covers all the basic router styles, along with how-it-works descriptions of all its major features. Includes sections on bits and accessories as well as square-cutting and trimming, case and furniture routing, cutting circles and arcs, template and freehand routing, and using the router with a router table. 128 pages.

Router Handbook. With nearly 600 illustrations of every conceivable bit, attachment, jig, and fixture, plus every possible operation, this definitive guide has revolutionized router applications. It begins with safety and maintenance tips, then forges ahead into all aspects of dovetailing, freehanding, advanced duplication, and more. Details for over 50 projects are included. 224 pages.

Router Jigs & Techniques. A practical encyclopedia of information, covering the latest equipment to use with your router, it describes all the newest of commercial routing machines, along with jigs, bits, and other aids and devices. The book not only provides invaluable tips on how to determine the router and bits best suited to your needs, but tells you how to get the most out of your equipment once it is bought. Over 800 photos and illustrations. 383 pages.

Scroll Saw Basics. This overview features more than 275 illustrations covering basic techniques and accessories. Sections include types of saw, features, selection of blades, safety, and how to use patterns. A half-dozen patterns are included to help the scroll saw user get started. Basic cutting techniques are covered, including inside cuts, bevel cuts, stack-sawing, and others. 128 pages.

Scroll Saw Country Patterns. With 300 full-size patterns in 28 categories, this selection of projects covers an extraordinary range with instruction every step of the way. Projects include cutouts of farm animals, people, birds, and butterflies, plus letter and key holders, coasters, switch plates, country hearts—and many more. The instruction provided includes piercing, drilling, sanding, and finishing, as well as tips on using special tools. 4 pages in color. 196 pages.

Scroll Saw Fretwork Patterns. This companion book to *Scroll Saw Fretwork Techniques & Projects* features over 200 fabulous full-size fretwork patterns. These patterns drawn by James Reidle include the most popular classic designs of the past, plus an array of imaginative contemporary ones. Choose from a variety of numbers, signs, brackets, animals, miniatures, and silhouettes, and many more. 256 pages.

Scroll Saw Fretwork Techniques & Projects. This companion book to *Scroll Saw Fretwork Patterns* offers a study in the historical development of fretwork, as well as the tools, techniques, materials, and project styles that have evolved over the past 130 years. Every intricate turn and cut is explained with over 550 step-by-step photos and illustrations. Patterns for all 32 projects are shown in full color. The book also covers some modern scroll-sawing machines as well as current state-of-the-art fretwork and fine scroll-sawing techniques. 8 pages in color. 232 pages.

Scroll Saw Handbook. This companion volume to *Scroll Saw Pattern Book* covers the essentials of this versatile tool, including the basics (how scroll saws work, blades to use, etc.) and the advantages and disadvantages of the general types and specific brand-name models available on the market. All cutting techniques are detailed, including compound and bevel sawing, making inlays, reliefs, and recesses, cutting metals and other nonwoods, and marquetry. There's even a section on transferring patterns to wood! Over 500 illustrations. 256 pages.

Scroll Saw Holiday Patterns. Mr. and Mrs. Spielman provide over 100 full-size, shaded patterns for easy cutting, plus full-color photos of projects. This book will serve all your holiday pleasures—all year long. These holiday patterns can be used for decorations, centerpieces, mailboxes, and a whole range of practical and gift ideas. Standard holidays, as well as the four seasons, birthdays, and anniversaries, are represented. 8 pages of color. 168 pages.

Scroll Saw Pattern Book. This companion book to *Scroll Saw Handbook* contains over 450 workable patterns for making wall plaques, refrigerator magnets, candle holders, pegboards, jewelry, ornaments, shelves, brackets, picture frames, signboards, and many more projects. Beginners and experienced scroll saw users alike will find something to intrigue and challenge them. 256 pages.

Scroll Saw Puzzle Patterns. 80 full-size patterns for jigsaw puzzles, standup puzzles, and inlay puzzles. With meticulous attention to detail, Patrick and Patricia Spielman provide instruction and step-by-step photos, along with tips on tools and wood selections, for making standup puzzles in the shape of dinosaurs, camels, hippopotamuses, alligators—even a family of elephants! Inlay puzzle patterns include basic shapes, numbers, an accurate piece-together map of the United States, and a host of other colorful educational and enjoyable games for children. 8 pages of color. 264 pages.

Scroll Saw Shelf Patterns. Spielman and master scroll saw designer Loren Raty offer full-size patterns for 44 different shelf styles. Designs include wall shelves, corner shelves, and multitiered shelves. The patterns work well with ¼-inch hardwood plywood or any select solid wood. Over 150 illustrations. 4 pages in color. 132 pages.

Scroll Saw Silhouette Patterns. With over 120 designs, Spielman and James Reidle provide a diverse collection of intricate silhouette patterns. Patterns range from Victorian themes to sports to cowboys. They also include animals, birds, and nautical designs as well as dragons, cars, and Christmas themes. Tips, hints, and advice are included along with detailed photos of finished works. 128 pages.

Sharpening Basics. This overview goes well beyond the "basics" to become a major up-to-date reference work featuring more than 300 detailed illustrations (mostly photos) to explain every facet of tool sharpening. Sections include bench-sharpening tools, sharpening machines, and safety. Chapters cover cleaning tools and sharpening all sorts of tools including chisels, plane blades (irons), hand knives, carving tools, turning tools, drill and boring tools, router and shaper tools, jointer and planer knives, drivers and scrapers, and, of course, saws. 144 pages.

Spielman's Original Scroll Saw Patterns. 262 full-size patterns that don't appear elsewhere feature teddy bears, dinosaurs, sports figures, dancers, cowboy cutouts, Christmas ornaments, and dozens more. Fretwork patterns are included for a Viking ship, framed cutouts, wall-hangers, key-chain miniatures, jewelry, self-decoration, and much more. Hundreds of step-by-step photos and drawings show how to flop, repeat, and crop each design for thousands of variations. 4 pages of color. 228 pages.

Victorian Gingerbread: Patterns & Techniques. Authentic pattern designs (many full-size) cover the full range of indoor and outdoor detailing: brackets, corbels, shelves, grilles, spandrels, balusters, running trim, headers, valances, gable ornaments, screen doors, pickets, trellises, and much more. Also included are complete plans for Victorian mailboxes, house numbers, signage, and more. With clear instructions and helpful drawings by James Reidle throughout, the book also provides tips for making your own gingerbread trim. 8 pages in color. 200 pages.

Victorian Scroll Saw Patterns. Intricate original designs plus classics from the 19th century are presented in full-size, shaded patterns. Instructions are provided with drawings and photos. The projects include alphabets and numbers, silhouettes and designs for shelves, frames, filigree baskets, plant holders, decorative boxes, picture frames, welcome signs, architectural ornaments, and much more. 192 pages.

Working Green Wood with PEG. Covers every process for making beautiful, inexpensive projects from green wood without cracking, splitting, or warping. Hundreds of clear photos and drawings show every step from obtaining the raw wood through shaping, treating, and finishing your PEG-treated projects. 175 unusual project ideas. Lists supply sources. 160 pages.

Index